To : someone very
adopted me i...

We want share with you...
Martin some pictures of new
town.
Our best wishes for this new year.
Daniel + Erika
x x x

Ian Cooper's
Orkney
in *Photographs*

Published by The Orcadian (Kirkwall Press)
Hell's Half Acre, Kirkwall, Orkney, KW15 1DW
Tel: 01856 879000   Fax: 01856 879001
www.orcadian.co.uk

Pictures: Ian Cooper   Words: James Miller

ISBN No: 978-1-902957-36-4

Printed by The Orcadian, Hatston Print Centre,
Hell's Half Acre, Kirkwall, Orkney, Scotland, KW15 1DW

Ian Cooper is an Orcadian, born and bred in Kirkwall.

After leaving school, 'Coop' has been in a variety of jobs but he is possibly best known among Orcadians as an accomplished musician.

He has played bass, acoustic and lead guitar at venues throughout Britain and partnered fellow Orcadian Ivan Drever in the Know O'Deil Band.

At the end of the 80's he became interested in photography and developed a hobby into a profession.

He has specialised in product photography and has been engaged by a number of local companies to compile photographic portfolios of their products.

Ring of Brodgar. The Ring of Brodgar, part of the Heart of Neolithic Orkney World Heritage Site, is one of the islands' most impressive monuments.

The ring – or henge – of upright stones form a perfect circle with a diameter of 340 feet; the stones themselves varying from 7 to 15 feet in height.

There were originally 60 standing stones but only 27 now remain.

The ring is thought to date back to 2500 – 2000BC and the position of the stones is reckoned to have astronomical significance.

St Magnus Cathedral. Work to build a Viking cathedral in Kirkwall, on the shore of the Peerie Sea, started in 1137 on the orders of Earl Rognvald Kolsson in memory of his uncle, Earl Magnus, who had been murdered on the island of Egilsay.

Both men were later canonised and their remains were laid to rest in two pillars within the building.

The cathedral is owned by the people of Orkney, not the church, and the building is managed on their behalf by Orkney Islands Council. The Society for the Friends of St Magnus raises funds for the upkeep of the building and there is an ongoing programme of repairs and restoration to the red sandstone.

Papa Westray. Orkney is rich in historic and archaeological sites but one of the less famous is the Knap of Howar on the fertile island of Papa Westray, in the North Isles.

The Neolithic site dates back to 3600 BC and contains one of the oldest – if not *the* oldest – standing houses in Western Europe. It is thought that the area was populated for around 500 years, the inhabitants no doubt attracted to the island because of its rich soil for farming and plentiful supply of birds on the cliffs.

Papa Westray is a popular destination for modern-day visitors to Orkney and the RSPB North Hill reserve is home to a variety of breeding birds including, guillemots, razorbills and kittiwakes. On the hill, a large colony of arctic terns nests close to arctic skuas, eiders, ringed plovers and oystercatchers.

Dark Green Fritillary. This butterfly was probably thinly distributed through the islands up until the last few years of the 20th century but, rather worryingly, sightings have become fewer and fewer and they can only now be found at one locality, the Bu sands in Burray.

Tim Dean, author of *The Orkney Book of* Birds, says "The food plant of the caterpillar is usually the Common Dog-violet of which there is an abundance in the county. Those Dark Green Fritillaries that live in Orkney are dark examples and belong to the subspecies *scotica.* They are single brooded and are on the wing from mid June to early August. In Britain it is the most widespread of the eight resident fritillary butterflies and can be found in a range of flower-rich grasslands."

Longhope. The Longhope Lifeboat Museum at Brims, near to Longhope, was established in 2000 and officially opened two years later by the Princess Royal, patron of the museum trust.

The museum is housed in the old station and slipway, and exhibits include the *Thomas McCunn*, a Watson-design lifeboat which was previously stationed in Longhope.

Tragedy struck the small community on March 17, 1969, when the Longhope lifeboat *T.G.B.* overturned during a rescue attempt and the eight-man crew perished. The lifeboat was alerted at 7.40pm when the Liberian cargo ship *Irene* got into trouble in the Pentland Firth in heavy seas and Force 9 gales. She subsequently grounded half a mile south of Grim Ness in South Ronaldsay and the entire crew was rescued by Coastguards.

The lifeboat, *T.G.B.*, with Coxswain Dan Kirkpatrick in charge, was last sighted around 9.30pm by a lighthouse keeper in very rough seas in the Firth. The last officially recorded message from her was received by Wick Radio at 9.28pm.

Around 1pm the following day the lifeboat was discovered overturned four miles south of Tor Ness and she was towed to Scrabster in Caithness. Seven men were found inside, including Coxswain Kirkpatrick.

There is an impressive memorial to the crew in the Osmondwall Cemetery on Hoy.

Kirkwall Airport. Air services to Orkney are vital for communication and commerce, and the operator, Flybe, in conjunction with Loganair, provide regular daily flights to the major Scottish cities.

Loganair also operate an internal air network to the smaller Orkney islands and one flight, from Westray to Papa Westray, lasts only two minutes, the shortest scheduled airline service in the world.

The company has two distinctive Islander-type aircraft in a predominantly black livery. These aircraft are sponsored by Highland Park Scotch whisky, which is based at a distillery on the outskirts of Kirkwall. A second single malt whisky called Scapa is also produced in the islands.

Shapinsay. The island of Shapinsay lies north of Kirkwall and behind the picturesque little village of Balfour is the imposing sight of Balfour Castle, a baronial-style building, that dominates the skyline.

Shapinsay has a strong farming pedigree and the island organises a successful agricultural show every year to promote the reputation of local livestock.

During the 1800's, the island underwent a minor agricultural revolution when David Balfour, an energetic and ambitious laird, financed a land reform programme, introducing efficient, square, ten acre field units, separated by open drains. He tripled the size of the estate's cultivated land area to 2,250 acres and evidence of his initiatives can still be seen today with the island's straight, right-angled road network.

Elwick Bay provides a sheltered natural harbour and was a popular base for Viking mariners.

Earl's Palace, Kirkwall

Waulkmill Bay, Orphir

Betty Corrigall, Hoy. The lonely and poignant grave of Betty Corrigall lies near the main road in open moorland. The young girl hanged herself because of an unwanted pregnancy to a sailor in the 19th century. In those days, the manner of her death meant she could not be buried in consecrated ground, so her grave was dug on the parish boundary, miles from anywhere.

Her body was discovered many years later by peat cutters and, during the Second World War, locally-based servicemen tended her grave and made a small white fence. Later, a talented Hoy artist, Harry Berry, built a headstone and in 1976 a burial service was conducted to consecrate the ground.

Earl's Palace, Kirkwall. What remains of the impressive Earl's Palace lies in the centre of the town near to St Magnus Cathedral and the Bishop's Palace.

It was built in the early 1600's by the infamous Earl Patrick Stewart and has many fine features, including a huge Great Hall.

Patrick Stewart was a hated earl of Orkney who had a reputation for avarice and extravagance. He maltreated local people but came unstuck when he ran into financial difficulties. He was subsequently charged with treason and incarcerated in Edinburgh Castle. Five years later "Black Patie" was executed aged 40.

Patrick Stewart's palace passed through various hands during the next century but, despite its splendour, it was unoccupied and uninhabitable by the early 1700's and fifty years later the roof was stripped and removed.

Farming. Orkney has a fairly diverse economy but – aside from the Flotta oil terminal development – the principal industries are agriculture and tourism.

By sheer hard work and careful marketing, the islands have developed an enviable reputation for producing quality food, including prime beef, lamb, shellfish and even locally-made ice cream and fudge.

There is excellent pasture and soil for agriculture in the islands, but unpredictable and inclement weather can make farming a hazardous business. However, over the centuries resourceful Orcadians have tilled the land to feed their families and nowadays there is a thriving food and livestock export business.

Arts and Crafts. This is an industry that has grown steadily over the past 30 years and is now a major employer in the islands.

Jewellery, in particular, is a high value sector of the industry and Orcadian companies manufacture a wide range of expensive, quality goods, primarily in gold and silver. The size of the Orkney jewellery firms can vary from "one man" operations to over 100 employees.

Pictured is Peter Rowland, a manufacturer based in the parish of Orphir, who specialises in the design of one-off pieces, limited editions and commissions in gold, silver and other metals.

John Rae. John Rae is an Orcadian hero who made his name in Canada as an explorer in the 1800's. He is regarded by some as the finest Arctic pioneer but, unfortunately, he was never given the recognition he deserved. Quite the reverse, in fact, he was vilified by the establishment.

Rae's success in surveying the geography of northern Canada and surviving the atrocious weather conditions when doing "field work" was, in part, due to the fact he respected the culture of the Inuit Indians, learned from them, and adopted many of their survival skills. He dressed as an Inuit and this was despised by many of his British peers.

The quest to find a North West Passage through Canada was high on the agenda of the British authorities at the time and resulted in a number of expeditions, including the ill-fated Franklin Expedition.

Rae later published evidence he had received from native Indians about the fate of Franklin, including accounts that the crew had resorted to cannibalism in an effort to survive. These reports proved unacceptable to the British authorities and Franklin's widow, who ran a highly successful campaign to discredit Rae.

In fact, Rae was the first to identify and map the last navigable channel of the Passage in 1854 and Roald Amundsen, who was the first to successfully navigate the entire route, described Rae's work as of "incalculable value".

Many believe that Rae deserves the title of 'Discoverer of the North West Passage'.

This powerful memorial to Rae is situated in St Magnus Cathedral.

JOHN RAE MD LLD FRS FRGS
ARCTIC EXPLORER
INTREPID DISCOVERER OF THE FATE OF SIR JOHN FRANKLIN'S LAST EXPEDITION
BORN 1813 DIED 1893
EXPEDITIONS 1846-47 1848-49 1851 1853-4

HMS *Royal Oak.* The memorial to HMS *Royal Oak* in St Magnus Cathedral, which includes the ship's bell, is a poignant reminder of a dark day in Orkney's history.

On the evening of October 13, 1939, the battleship was moored safely – or so everyone thought – in her Scapa Flow anchorage when a German U-boat struck and sent the ageing battleship to the bottom with the loss of 833 crew members.

The German submarine, *U47*, commanded by Gunther Prien, had penetrated the defences of the Royal Navy anchorage by slipping past blockships in the Kirk Sound channel, next to where the Italian Chapel is now situated.

It is thought that the *Royal Oak* took just 15 minutes to sink and Prien made a successful escape out into open sea and back to Germany, where he was acclaimed a national hero by Hitler.

The attack prompted Churchill to demand better protection for the fleet base and resulted in the construction of four concrete barriers to block off routes into the Flow.

The wreck of the *Royal Oak* is now an official war grave and Royal Navy divers place a White Ensign flag on the hulk each year, in memory of those who perished.

Click Mill, Dounby. The last surviving horizontal water mill in Orkney is located near Dounby in the West Mainland.

The mill takes its name from the clicking sound it made when in operation.

The design is of Norse origins and the mill is maintained by Historic Scotland and is open to the public.

Buttercup fields, looking east over Orphir

Birsay coast and Brough

Hoy. Hackness Martello Tower and Battery is one of two constructed in Hoy after 1813 to protect the entrance to Longhope, during the Napoleonic Wars. The other tower is at Crockness and they were armed with 24 pounder cannons.

British ships at the time were not only under threat from the French but also American naval and private raiders, and Longhope was regarded as a safe haven for mariners heading for the Baltic or taking a northerly route around Britain in order to avoid the English Channel.

The walls of the towers are up to 3 metres thick and the towers were even used for defence purposes in both World Wars.

The Hackness tower has been substantially restored by Historic Scotland.

Finstown. This view from the top of Wideford Hill looks westwards to the village of Finstown and the parish of Firth.

The village takes its name from the surname of an Irish soldier and Napoleonic Wars veteran, called Phin, who opened up an inn, in what is now the heart of the village.

Phin was reputed to be a great storyteller and his inn, The Toddy Hole, grew in popularity.

To the right in the picture is the island of Grimbister.

The Ba'. On Christmas and New Year's Days the narrow streets of Kirkwall are jammed packed with people for the Ba'.

This is an ancient street ball game, but with no rules, other than the two sides – the Uppies and Doonies – have to touch a cork-filled leather ball at a goal, at either end of the town, in order to win the contest. The game is extremely physical and not for the faint hearted.

Four games are played during the festive period, two each for men and boys, and generate huge excitement among a vocal crowd of supporters.

The men's game usually lasts several hours and, once the game has been settled, the winning side has an internecine debate to "elect" a winner, who is allowed to keep the ba'.

Blockships. The sinking of HMS *Royal Oak* in Scapa Flow by a German U-boat and the loss of 833 sailors in 1939 shocked the British authorities to the core. A major improvement in the defences around Orkney was ordered by the Government and resulted, amongst other things, in the construction of the Churchill Barriers.

Up until the sinking of the *Royal Oak,* the defences around Scapa Flow were woefully inadequate and principally comprised of sunken blockships, scuttled in channels leading into the anchorage from open sea.

The remains of many of these blockships can still be seen today, particularly when crossing the Churchill Barriers at low tide.

Birsay. The parish of Birsay derives its name from the Norse and suggests "fortification", possibly alluding to the Brough of Birsay, the site of an ancient settlement.

Not far from the Brough is the ruinous Earl's Palace, which was built by one of the hated Stewart dynasty of Orkney earls.

Built in the 1570/80's in two phases, it would have been a very grand building of the times and comprised two storeys, a great hall, and three towers.

A 1633 account of the building described it as "sumptuous and stately".

The ruin is looked after by Historic Scotland and is open to the public.

Air Services, This modern day picture of a De Havilland Dragon aircraft on an Orkney runway is a throwback to the past when air services in and out of the islands dominated the news.

The 1920's and 30's were a golden time for young aviators, and Orkney was at the centre of the new age as budding pioneers, attempting transatlantic crossings by air, used the islands as a staging post.

Capt "Ted" Fresson became the founder of air services in the north of Scotland. In 1931, he came to Orkney offering short airborne pleasure trips and, within two years, he formed Highland Airways Ltd. On May 8, 1933, he completed the first scheduled flight from Inverness (via Wick) to Orkney and landed at Wideford, close to the present Kirkwall Airport. *The Orcadian* newspaper acted as his agent in Orkney.

The service proved popular and, within months, the company announced the introduction of a De Havilland Dragon, an eight-seater aircraft.

Further achievements came a year later for Fresson: he was given the first domestic airmail contract by the Postmaster General, allowing post from Orkney to reach London in 18 hours; and then he started Britain's first air ambulance service.

There is a small memorial to Fresson at Wideford, beside the main road leading from the airport into Kirkwall.

Lyness, Hoy. Lyness was at the very heart of Scapa Flow activities during both World Wars.

While the Flow was an ideal natural anchorage, Lyness provided a perfect base and the authorities spent vast sums of money on developing the site to provide the necessary infrastructure for an efficient headquarters, including underground oil storage tanks, harbours and even a railway.

A poignant reminder that the tragedy of war does not recognise national borders is the naval cemetery at Lyness, where headstones mark the graves of war dead, including Germans killed during the scuttle of the interned German High Seas Fleet in Scapa Flow after the First World War.

The German scuttle was the largest loss of shipping in a single day in history. Four hundred thousand tons of warships were sunk, comprising five battle cruisers, 10 battleships, five cruisers and 31 other ships.

Needless to say, there followed a massive salvage operation which is a story in itself.

The Scapa Flow Visitor Centre is located at Lyness and is well worth a visit.

Hoxa World War defences, South Ronaldsay

The Strynd, Kirkwall

The **Gloup, Deerness.** The Gloup is what remains of a collapsed coastal cave and provides a dramatic example of sea power during the winter, when water surges in through the narrow entrance.

It is a more passive spectacle (usually!) in the summer months but visitors should exercise extreme caution when going to the site and use the footpaths and viewing bridge.

The Gloup is approximately 50 yards long and 80 feet deep and can be accessed by small boat in favourable sea conditions.

Fishermen's Huts. Orkney's many coves and "geos" provide excellent shelter and landing places for fishermen, particularly in rough winter weather.

Fine examples can be found at Skipi Geo and Sand Geo in Birsay and the fishermen's huts, pictured, were restored in the 1980's with the help of local schoolchildren.

While fishing has always provided Orkney inhabitants with a valuable food source, it is said that Orcadians are "Farmers who fish", whereas Shetlanders are "Fishermen who farm".

Skipi Geo, near to the Brough of Birsay, and Sand Geo, close to Marwick Bay, are popular destinations for people who enjoy a short walk.

North Ronaldsay. The most northerly island in the Orkney archipelago, North Ronaldsay, is home to a rare breed of sheep.

North Ronaldsay sheep are unique. They are retained on the beach by a drystane dyke, that goes around the entire island, and live on seaweed, except in the spring, when ewes and lambs are allowed on grassland for three or four months.

The diet of the small sheep gives their meat a very distinctive flavour.

Hoxa, **South Ronaldsay.** Orkney's strategic importance during both World Wars cannot be overstated and particularly that of the sheltered naval anchorage of Scapa Flow.

In fact, during the Second World War, Orkney was fortified to such an extent that, outside London, it had one of the biggest defence networks in the country.

Any visitor to Orkney cannot fail to see the remains of huge, abandoned concrete lookout posts and gun emplacements but what most people see is only the tip of the iceberg as much has been removed or is located in inaccessible or remote spots.

The gun emplacement pictured here, under a dark, threatening sky, is at Hoxa in South Ronaldsay, at the very entrance to the Flow.

Burwick. Any summer visitor to Orkney would be extremely unlucky if they did not witness an impressive sunset such as this one at Burwick, on the southernmost tip of South Ronaldsay.

Burwick looks out on to the Pentland Firth – where the Atlantic Ocean and North Sea meet – and a popular foot passenger ferry plies from Caithness during the summer months. There were ambitious plans in the 1980's for a major ferry terminal to be built in the area to provide a "short sea crossing" but, so far, it has failed to materialise.

Pentland Ferries run a vehicular ferry service from St Margaret's Hope (also is South Ronaldsay) to Gills Bay in Caithness.

Castle of Yesnaby. The west coast of Orkney has arguably the most picturesque coastal scenery in the county. Walking from Stromness to Costa offers some breathtaking cliff-top sights and any keen rambler will be greatly rewarded for their strenuous efforts.

One of the highlights – and more accessible areas – is Yesnaby, where visitors can see this stack after a short walk from the public car park. There are several other impressive sea stacks in the area.

Skara Brae. The ancient village of Skara Brae, in the parish of Sandwick, is one of the most outstanding monuments in the world.

The Neolithic village, a tight group of dwelling houses, lies on the edge of Skaill Bay and was first uncovered in 1850, after a storm. The structures had been preserved in sand and, when meaningful excavations were made in the late 1920's, the magnitude and importance of the discovery was realised.

Modern dating methods now estimate that the village dates back to 3200BC – 2200BC.

An interpretation centre for visitors – with a "as it was" replica – is near to the site.

Hoy Sound from the Black Craig

Typical Orcadian coastline in winter

St Rognvald Chapel. The chapel is situated within St Magnus Cathedral, below the towering and magnificent East Window or Rose Window, which faces east.

The chapel was designed by the Orcadian artist Stanley Cursiter and a local craftsman, Reynold Eunson, and features handsome wooden figures depicting the "Founding Fathers" of the cathedral, Earl Rognvald, his father, Kol, and Bishop William.

Cursiter was appointed the Queen's Painter and Limner for Scotland and was later made a Freeman of Kirkwall. He died in 1976.

The East Window is dedicated to Sheriff Thoms, who left £60,000 for renovation and repairs to the Cathedral from 1913-30.

Orphir. The Hall of Clestrain dates back to the 1760's and was the birthplace of John Rae, an Orcadian Arctic explorer who discovered the final, key channel of the North West Passage, a sea route through northern Canada.

Sadly, he did not receive the recognition he deserved, as he was ridiculed by the authorities for reporting that crew members from the ill-fated John Franklin Expedition had resorted to cannibalism.

His home on the shores of Scapa Flow is in a poor state of repair but there are plans to locate an Orkney Boat Museum in the area and include the house as part of the development.

Ward Hill, Hoy. A wintery scene at Scorrabrae, with a derelict cottage in the foreground, and Scapa Flow and the Hoy Hills, to the rear.

The landscape of Hoy is the nearest in appearance that Orkney gets to the Scottish Highlands and, in the centre of this picture, is a snow-dusted Ward Hill, the islands' highest hill at 1,565 feet above sea level.

Italian Chapel. The Italian Chapel on the island of Lamb Holm is known throughout the world.

After Churchill ordered the defences of Scapa Flow to be reinforced in 1939 and the building of inter-island barriers, 550 Italian prisoners of war were shipped to Orkney from North Africa to provide much needed labour. It was illegal for prisoners to be deployed on military-related work so, rather neatly for the British, they were used in the construction of *causeways*.

The POWs appealed for the provision of a chapel in which to worship and, once permission was granted by their captors, set about converting a Nissen hut. The prisoners and a man named Domenico Chiocchetti, in particular, salvaged what materials they could from around Camp 60 and slowly, but surely, realised their dream.

The result is what we see today; a beautifully ornate and moving symbol of war and peace.

Old Man of Hoy. Orkney's oldest inhabitant is situated on the west coast of the island, and visitors arriving on a Stromness-bound ferry get an early introduction to him en route.

Hoy is Norse for High Island and it is easy to see why.

The Old Man is the tallest sea stack in Britain at 449 feet (137m) and, although it was only first climbed in 1966 by a team which included Chris Bonington, it is now scaled on a regular basis.

The path to the Old Man starts at Rackwick Bay and is almost four miles long, over fairly rough moorland. Walkers will also, in all probability, be "dive bombed" by great skuas, or "bonxies"!

Orkney Ferries. The islands' internal ferry service is run by the local authority, Orkney Islands Council, through a company called Orkney Ferries.

The company has a fleet of eight roll-on, roll-off (or "ro-ro") vehicle ferries and one passenger-only boat, serving 13 islands, from various embarkation points on the Orkney Mainland.

The service is very frequent but during the summer months it is advisable to book vehicles in advance.

The two ferries pictured, the *Earl Sigurd* and *Earl Thorfinn*, serve the North Isles and are the biggest vessels in the fleet.

Puffins. Puffins, with their highly-coloured and distinctive beaks, are a hugely popular attraction for visitors to Orkney.

Tim Dean, in his excellent *The Orkney Books of Birds*, writes "apart from their colourful and patterned clown-faces that present an expression of sadness, doom and depression, they usually allow the visitor a confiding intimacy that most other birds do not."

"They are primarily burrowers but can also be found tenanting holes and crevices in cliff faces."

They can be observed on many Mainland locations but they prefer offshore islands and Orkney's largest colony is on uninhabited Sule Skerry, where there are 60,000 occupied burrows.

Sheep wall, North Ronaldsay

Sunset at Aikerness, Evie

Rackwick Bay. For many Orcadians, Orkney's finest spot is Rackwick Bay in Hoy; a magnificent, sweeping, boulder-strewn bay, with towering red sandstone cliffs, several miles from the Old Man of Hoy.

The area can be reached by car but, for many, the magic of Rackwick can only be fully appreciated after taking the short ferry ride from Stromness to Moaness and then trekking through the valley in the shadow of Ward Hill.

Sandwick. Skaill House is a fine example of a 17th century Orkney laird's mansion.

Situated near to the prehistoric village of Skara Brae, it takes its name from the Norse *skali*, "Old Hall" or main farm building, and it is believed that the area has been continuously cultivated for a thousand years.

The house is open to the public and is presented as it was in the 1950's.

Dwarfie Stane. Not far from the road to Rackwick Bay in Hoy, below the Dwarfie Hamars, is the Dwarfie Stane.

It is the only north European example of a rock tomb, with a small passage and two chambers. A large boulder, which was once used to seal the entrance, can also be identified.

The stone got its name from the Norsemen, who believed that it was a home for dwarfs.

South Ronaldsay. The pretty village of St Margaret's Hope is situated on the island of South Ronaldsay and is known locally simply as "The 'Hope", which derives from the Norse "small bay".

The village has a maritime history and was used as a sheltered anchorage by Vikings. It only really developed, however, in 1840, when the fishing industry boomed and 245 herring boats worked the surrounding area.

There is a romantic notion that the village takes its name from the unfortunate Margaret, Maid of Norway, who died in 1290.

At the nearby Sands of Wright the Boys' Ploughing Match, or Festival of the Horse, takes place each year. It is an old tradition whereby children dress up in decorative horse harnesses and the boys compete at ploughing with mini ploughs on the beach.

Short-eared Owl. "The sight of a honey-coloured Short-eared Owl hunting over rough fields or perched atop a roadside post is always guaranteed to uplift the grimmest of moods" according to Tim Dean in *The Orkney Book of Birds*.

"Most owls are abroad at night, but the '*cattie-face*' can be seen during daylight throughout the county and for most of the year. It is during winter when they become a little bit harder to see; the longer winter nights mean that they become more nocturnal.

"Additionally, research has shown that some birds leave Orkney altogether – most probably head for the mainland of Scotland but a chick that was ringed in Firth during May 1983 was shot in the following October in the Basque region of Spain. Nests are made in heather and rushes during May and often the parents raise two or even three youngsters. Owl activity is at its greatest in June and July when the young are at their most demanding."

Seals. Seals are a very common sight in Orkney and visitors to the islands at any time of the year are sure to see them at some point.

In fact, 25,000 grey seals live in the waters around Orkney, a significant proportion of the estimated worldwide population of 290,000. There are fewer common seals (pictured) but there are still believed to be 7,000 in the vicinity.

Corrigall Farm Museum, Harray. There are two farm museums in Orkney, at Corrigall in Harray (pictured) and Kirkbuster in Birsay.

The Corrigall museum features a typical Orkney farmhouse in mid 19th century appearance, a working barn and grain kiln, horse-drawn machinery and livestock.

"The old house at Kirkbuster has survived at least four centuries, complete with its central hearth ... the only one of its kind in Northern Europe.   It is higher and wider, and is richer in windows than the traditional 'black house' usually associated with central hearth" according to the museum's Katrina Mainland.

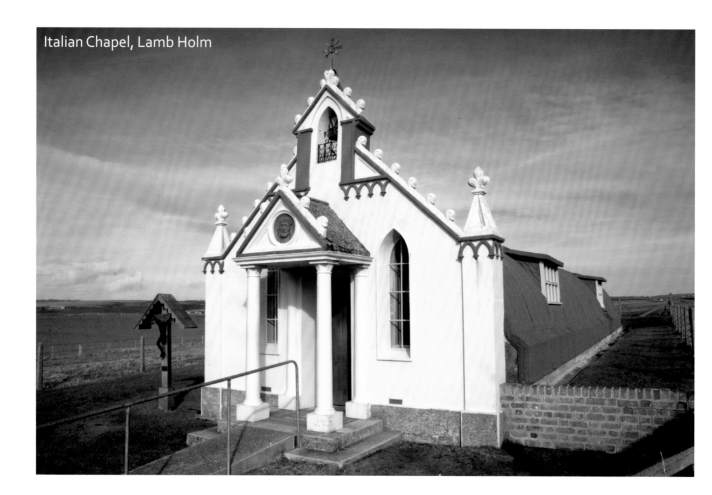
Italian Chapel, Lamb Holm

Cruise liners. Tourism in Orkney is a vital component of the local economy and over the past thirty years much work has gone into promoting the islands as a cruise liner destination.

This has paid dividends and now, from spring through to the early autumn, it is common to see cruise liners berthed at the new Kirkwall harbour, or anchored in the bay. The ships usually arrive overnight and passengers spend a full day on the Mainland, visiting the historic sites and shopping.

Stromness. Stromness is the smaller of Orkney's two towns and is the arrival port for the islands' principal ferry link with the Scottish mainland.

Nestled under Wardhill, or Brinkies Brae, it offers a picturesque welcome to ferry passengers arriving from Scrabster and its cobbled streets and quaint little lanes, make it a town of considerable charm and character.

Hamnavoe (haven bay) as it was once known, developed as a port in the 1600's, supplying passing ships en route around Britain or heading west to Canada, to open up new frontiers. Ships from the Hudson's Bay Co. called at Stromness extensively and, by 1817, the town had 38 ale houses to quench the thirst of parched seamen.

Stromness was the home to one of Orkney's famous sons, the writer George Mackay Brown, who died in 1996.

Flotta. Pictured is a wartime entrance to the naval anchorage of Scapa Flow, viewed from Hoxa Head on South Ronaldsay across to the island of Flotta.

Flotta was at the centre of military activity during both World Wars but now it is home to a large oil terminal, which is linked by pipeline to the North Sea oilfields. Tankers come into the safe waters of the Flow to collect their cargo.

The discovery of North Sea oil was a welcome boost to the local economy, providing employment to Orcadians and income to the Orkney Harbours Authority, which is subsequently used by the local council to encourage economic development.

Stenness. A little beauty spot, known locally as "Happy Valley" can be found in the parish of Stenness.

It is actually the garden of a cottage, Banksburn, and was created over many years by Edwin Harrold, who died in 2005.

Like much of Orkney, the area was treeless and Mr Harrold slowly developed a small woodland and garden paradise around a nearby burn. Living without electricity, hot water and television for most of his life, he spent his spare time tending his creation and welcoming visitors to his garden.

Festivals. Over the past thirty-five years a number of festivals have been established and Orkney now hosts an event nearly every month of the summer. They include the St Magnus Festival and Magfest (pictured) which is devoted to music and the arts, a folk festival and even an international science festival.

In 1977, the St Magnus Festival was founded by a group led by Sir Peter Maxwell Davies and it has grown into one of Britain's "most highly regarded and adventurous arts events". Sir Peter lives in Orkney and is Master of the Queen's Music.

NorthLink. The *Hamnavoe*, pictured sailing into Stromness from Scrabster, provides a daily ferry service to Orkney and is owned by a publicly-subsidised company called NorthLink, which also provides a ferry service to Shetland.

The company, which also sails out of Aberdeen, has a fleet of two other passenger vessels, *Hjaltland*, and *Hrossey*, and two freight vessels, *Hascosay* and *Clare*.

The state-subsidised "lifeline service" to the northern island groups was previously provided by P & O Ferries. A Gills Bay to St Margaret's Hope route is operated by the privately-owned Pentland Ferries.

Churchill Barriers. The Churchill Barriers (or causeways) link four islands to the Orkney Mainland and were built during the Second World War to safeguard the naval anchorage of Scapa Flow for the British fleet.

The order to build them was triggered by the sinking of the battleship *Royal Oak* at her mooring in the Flow, in 1939, by a German U-boat. The German submarine commander, Gunther Prien, slipped past the inadequate British defences and through the Kirk Sound channel, pictured, under cover of darkness.

The causeway pictured is known as Number One Barrier and links the island of Lamb Holm, where the Italian Chapel is situated, with the parish of Holm (pronounced "Ham") on the Mainland.

Kirbister Loch, Orphir

Marinas. In recent years Orkney has promoted itself as a yachting destination and there are now three established marinas in Kirkwall (pictured), Stromness and Westray.

The modern facilities have a total of more than 170 berths and have attracted yachtsmen from all over the world, particularly the Scandinavian countries.

The initiative has been so successful that there are plans to develop and expand the facilities.

Standing Stones of Stenness. Just over a mile along the road from the Ring of Brodgar are the Standing Stones of Stenness.

These stones originally formed a ring of 12 and, at heights up to 19 feet, are considerably taller than the ones at Brodgar. It is believed that the position of the stones have lunar and solar significance.

Sadly, a number of years ago some of the stones were removed by a local farmer, including The Stone of Odin. This megalith had a hole, and lovers clasped hands though it to pledge their undying love for each other.

Dated at 3000BC, it is one of the earliest stone circles in Britain.

Kirkwall. The capital of Orkney is the City and Royal Burgh of Kirkwall.

The town is considerably larger than Stromness and is the administrative centre of the islands, with the Orkney Islands Council headquarters situated near to St Magnus Cathedral, which dominates the skyline.

A narrow street runs through the town from the harbour, where a wide assortment of ferries, fishing boats and pleasure craft are moored in the "Basin", pictured.

The town has a very active commercial centre, with a wide variety of local shops, and there is a large industrial estate on the outskirts, at Hatston, once the site of a Second World War aerodrome.

The town takes its name from the Norse Kirkjuvagr, "kirk on the bay".

Maeshowe. There are chambered cairns all over the Orkney Islands but the biggest and best known is Maeshowe in the parish of Stenness, alongside the main Kirkwall to Stromness road.

The cairn is precisely positioned so that the setting sun at the winter solstice (and for several weeks at that time) shines down the long entrance passage and on to the back wall of the tomb.

The monument, which dates back to 2700BC, was broken into by Vikings, who left runic inscriptions – or graffiti – on the walls. They tell stories of their women and, intriguingly, hidden treasure.

The Brig o' Waithe. The Brig o' Waithe is at the mouth of the Loch of Stenness.

In March 1940, Germans bombers appeared over Scapa Flow, the Royal Navy base, and were engaged by British fighters. The Germans jettisoned their high explosive and incendiary bombs near to the brig and killed a local man, who was standing in the doorway of his house.

James Isbister, aged 27, became the first British civilian air raid casualty of World War Two.

Index